FRIEDRICH SCHLEIERMACHER

DATE DUE

MAKERS OF CONTEMPORARY THEOLOGY

EDITORS:
The Rev. Professor D. E. Nineham
The Rev. E. H. Robertson

PAUL TILLICH, *by Heywood Thomas*
RUDOLF BULTMANN, *by Ian Henderson*
DIETRICH BONHOEFFER, *by E. H. Robertson*
TEILHARD DE CHARDIN, *by Bernard Towers*
MARTIN BUBER, *by Ronald Gregor Smith*
GABRIEL MARCEL, *by Sam Keen*
MARTIN HEIDEGGER, *by John Macquarrie*
LUDWIG WITTGENSTEIN, *by W. D. Hudson*
ALFRED NORTH WHITEHEAD, *by Norman Pittenger*
SÖREN KIERKEGAARD, *by Robert L. Perkins*

FRIEDRICH SCHLEIERMACHER

by

STEPHEN SYKES

Dean of St. John's College
Cambridge, England

LONDON
LUTTERWORTH PRESS

British edition published by the Lutterworth Press
4 Bouverie Street, London, England, 1971

American edition published by the John Knox Press,
Richmond, Virginia, U.S.A., 1971

First published 1971

ISBN 0 7188 1826 1

*Printed in Great Britain
by Lonsdale & Bartholomew (Bath) Ltd.*

Contents

Introduction

UNDERSTANDING the theology of a subtle theological writer is itself a theological task, and the division between 'life', 'thought' and 'significance', which this work adopts, must always be a little artificial. There is something about the work of an Augustine, an Aquinas or a Luther which challenges the theologian's whole approach to his subject; and if there is to be a figure from the nineteenth or twentieth centuries to stand in that company, it is more likely to be F. D. E. Schleiermacher than any other.

To write an introduction of 50 pages to an intellectual giant of this size poses problems which can only be solved by a rigorous limitation of aims. This introduction attempts to do no more, after a brief account of Schleiermacher's life, than probe two central themes of his theology. These, though they have been subjected to more than 100 years of scrutiny, are still widely misunderstood and misinterpreted. But they form a basis upon which the reader may, if he so chooses, embark on a study of Schleiermacher for himself.

A few of the more than thirty volumes of Schleiermacher's collected works are available in English and these are listed on p. 52. In practice, however, his influence has been chiefly felt through his speeches *On Religion*,[1] *The Christian Faith*,[2] and to a

---

[1] There are now two English translations of this work, hereafter referred to as *O.R.* Quotations in this book are from the most recent of these, by T. N. Tice (John Knox Press, 1969), which is a translation of the third German edition of 1821. The same edition was translated by John Oman in 1893 and is available as a Harper Torchbook (Harper and Row, 1958); it is still useful, and page references to it have been added in brackets.

[2] Translation edited in 1928 by H. R. Mackintosh and J. S. Stewart (T. and T. Clark), hereafter referred to as *C.F.*

lesser extent the *Brief Outline on the Study of Theology*.[3] This is not to deny that in other important respects, for example in the current interest in hermeneutics, Schleiermacher is not a highly significant figure. It nevertheless remains a fact that for the majority of English speaking students these are the works which they must be encouraged to read if they wish to come to grips *for themselves* with the foremost theological intellect of the nineteenth century.

Let there be no mistake. There is scarcely a subject, be it religious education, the Christian attitude to other religions, the structure of theology as an academic discipline or belief in Christ's resurrection, on which Schleiermacher does not write something balanced and penetrating for our own times. Reading and rereading him one is constantly delighted with the subtlety and insight of his mind. The attempt here is to lay out as clearly as possible, yet without distortion, the basic considerations from which his Christian theology sets out; and if the reader is encouraged to turn or return to Schleiermacher's own exposition, that will have been sufficient justification for writing.

[3] Translation by T. N. Tice (John Knox Press, 1966), hereafter referred to as *B.O.*

I

Life

Background

IN presenting Schleiermacher to an English speaking audience on both sides of the Atlantic, one is reminded of the passage in the 'Explanations' added in 1821 to his fourth speech *On Religion* where he bewails the fact that British influence seemed to be on the increase in the United States while German influence was declining. His remedy was wholesale immigration! For the British constitution, establishment and attitude to religion Schleiermacher had no sympathy whatsoever. In the United States, on the other hand, he expressed considerable interest and entertained some considerable hopes.

The fact was that Britain of the early nineteenth century did not seem to fit into the emerging pattern of European history and church life. It was a revolutionary era.

Schleiermacher (1768–1832) was born just before the American war of independence (1776–83); the industrial revolution of the eighteenth century was making its influence felt in Europe throughout his life; the French revolution broke out when he was ten, and he saw Prussia overrun by Napoleon when a university professor of 38. Whether or not we allow ourselves the liberty of saying that 'with these events the modern world began', we can scarcely doubt their importance.

With them Christianity also was to undergo its own revolutions. It had already experienced Renaissance and Reformation. The broadening of the intellectual horizons, the Protestant assertion of the individual's right to interpret the Scriptures and the disruption of the external spiritual unity of Christendom had all created by the seventeenth century a ferment of conflicting ideas.

The prestige of purely theological activity suffered irrevocably. The Thirty Years War (1618–48) in which Protestant and Catholic powers were at each other's throats, and the English Civil War of 1642–49 led sensitive people to doubt, more fundamentally than rational argument, whether all truth could be contained in one of the competing confessional creeds.

Rational argument was not slow to appear, however. Galileo Galilei (1564–1642) produced many of his works in this period, only to encounter the strong opposition of the Holy Office. René Descartes (1596–1650), one of the earliest philosophers to write in the vernacular rather than Latin, published his *Discourse on Method* in 1637, and tried throughout his philosophical activity to employ the principles and methods of mathematics. Lord Herbert of Cherbury (1583–1648) tried to define a common essence of religion, natural to all humanity and underlying the assertions of the individual dogmatic systems. The English Deists, who followed in his steps, further elaborated criticisms of the supernatural elements in Christianity and sought to free religion from what they felt to be superstitious and intolerant opinions. Works began to appear in England at the end of the seventeenth and at the beginning of the eighteenth centuries with titles like *Christianity not Mysterious*, *Discourse on Free-thinking*, and *Christianity as Old as Creation*.[4]

With the beginning of the eighteenth century and on the basis of such works, and those of the philosophers John Locke (1632–1704) and G. W. Leibniz (1646–1716), and of the mathematician and natural philosopher Isaac Newton (1643–1727), we are brought to the brink of that intellectual movement called the Enlightenment. This, like most general terms in intellectual history, is an omnibus word designed to convey a number of different meanings. But among them would unquestionably be included three; a strong confidence in the powers of human reason and natural enquiry to uncover the truth in every field; a

[4] For all these see L. Stephen, *History of English Thought in the Eighteenth Century*, I (1876), chs. ii-iv. Available as a Harbinger paperback (Harcourt, Brace and World Inc., 1963).

preparedness to open the area of discussion of religion beyond the categories of Christianity and Paganism to include the possibility of discovering a religion 'natural' to humanity; and pronounced educational and social aims designed to release the promise of development towards an enlightened order of society. Other characteristics of the Enlightenment could doubtless be added to expand the picture. And it must be emphasized that the characteristics mentioned are developed by the different leaders of these movements in ways which differ widely from each other.[5]

This movement of Enlightenment is the essential background to the proper appreciation of the religious situation in which Schleiermacher lived, despite the fact that other literary and philosophical movements enveloped it. Under its influence the whole Christian interpretation of the world and man, its doctrines and its social ramifications, was subjected (one can well say, is still subjected) to scrutiny and reappraisal.

The Enlightenment affected the Churches in different European countries in differing ways. In England, for example, the early Deists were not the only writers to reassess the relations of faith and reason, and there grew up within the Church a tradition both of scientific enquiry and of tolerant theology, known as 'Latitudinarianism'. When these freedoms were exported to Europe, however, they took on a different form and met with different reactions. The French writer, Voltaire (1694–1778), after a three-year exile in England, began to popularize the English Enlightenment in his works, *Lettres philosophiques sur les Anglais* (1734) and *Eléments de la Philosophie de Newton* (1738). Under Voltaire's influence, the Enlightenment in France developed in a pronouncedly anti-clerical direction. But it was in Germany that the Enlightenment, slow to take root, eventually effected the most radical and lasting transformation.

The early years of the German Enlightenment are characterized in the Protestant Churches by the parallel development of

[5] Some delightful portraits of leaders of the Enlightenment are contained in H. G. Nicholson's *The Age of Reason* (Constable & Co., 1960). Available also as a Panther paperback (1968).

rationalist orthodoxy, a rational defence of traditional theology, and of 'neology', an attempt to purge Christian doctrine of untenable superstitions and present the faith in a form palatable to the sceptical intelligentsia. But the great transformation of theology in Germany was accomplished less by the original leaders of the Enlightenment than by those of its new development, German Idealism, which took form largely in the critical years 1770–90. It is important initially to describe this development as continuous with the early Enlightenment. It accepted the aim, though not the methods, of its predecessor. It accepted the principle of human autonomy in all matters of a technical or scientific variety; and it desired, moreover, to restore in a total account of the world that principle of unity which theology had formerly supplied. But it was unwilling to give to enlightened reason alone the task of constructing and regulating this system.

The philosophy of Immanuel Kant (1724–1804), the literature of J. W. Goethe (1749–1832), and the various enterprises of the German Romantics, all played a part in creating a great revival of art, philosophy and literature, which has made an indelible impression upon modern thought, and not least modern theology. For German Idealism, while rooted in Protestantism, manifestly offered ways of viewing the world which were not identical with traditional Christianity. Was the Church's reaction to be outright rejection, partial compromise, or total capitulation? This was the pressing problem of the years in which Schleiermacher was receiving his education.

Family and Early Years

One rather striking picture of Schleiermacher's early life comes from his own pen; the high-flown style of expression is no more than an affectation of that particular book.

> Piety was, as it were, the maternal womb in whose sacred obscurity my young life was nourished and prepared for a world still closed to it. Before my spirit had found its distinctive sphere in the search for knowledge

and in the mature experience of life, it found its vital breath in piety. As I began to sift out the faith of my fathers and to clear the rubbish of former ages from my thoughts and feelings piety supported me. As the childhood images of God and immortality vanished before my doubting eyes piety remained.[6]

His father, a Reformed (Calvinist) minister, had fallen under the influence of 'piety' when Schleiermacher was only ten years old. This 'piety' was the pattern of religious life practised by the Herrnhuter, or Moravian Brethren as they are called in the English speaking world. Since this movement is of such lasting importance for Schleiermacher's development (he was prepared later in life to refer to himself as a Herrnhuter of a higher order) some account of it is necessary.

In structure the movement goes back to the Bohemian brethren of the fifteenth century. At the Reformation a part of this movement joined the Lutheran Church, and shortly afterwards settled in Moravia (in modern Czechoslovakia). After a further scattering in the seventeenth century, a group of exiles eventually settled in 1721 on the estate of Count N. L. von Zinzendorf at Berthelsdorf (in modern East Germany). The settlement was called Herrnhut, 'watch of the Lord', and grew to be an important and abiding influence on German Protestantism. In the newly reconstituted brotherhood two influences combined: the Moravian discipline of a pure, unworldly brotherhood of Christians under the close supervision of elders, and Zinzendorf's own strong pietism, as developed under the influence of P. J. Spener (1635-1705), Zinzendorf's godfather. This pietism expressed itself in the cultivation of an emotionally powerful devotional life and a sense of intimate fellowship with Christ, nourished by a discipline of meetings for prayer and Bible study. In England, John Wesley was strongly influenced by this movement, and visited Herrnhut in 1738.

This was the brotherhood to which Schleiermacher's father turned in 1778, and in whose pattern of religious life he found peace. Its influence upon Schleiermacher began at a most impressionable age. After a somewhat precocious start to his

[6] O.R., pp. 47-8 (9).

schooling, Schleiermacher's parents had the idea of handing over his further education, and that of all their children, to the brethren. Schleiermacher went first to a school in Gnadenfrei, a village south of Breslau (in modern Poland), then at the age of 14 to a college for future members of the brotherhood at Nieski (in modern Eastern Germany, near the Neisse border).

It is clear that he enjoyed and profited from his first years with the community, his mother's death in 1783 perhaps increasing his dependence upon it. But problems were to come. At the age of 16 he entered the theological seminary of the brethren in Barby, a town on the Elbe sixteen miles from Magdeburg (in modern Eastern Germany). Here theological education was combined with a certain suspicion of all new philosophical enterprises. Schleiermacher's questions were set aside with appeals to a faith founded on the inner testimony of the heart. The students were forbidden access to the new literature, with the consequence that many of them formed the suspicion that the objections there offered to belief must be most difficult to refute. Tension mounted in Schleiermacher's mind, until finally in an agonized letter to his father he confessed his far-reaching doubts. With such a confession his future with the brotherhood had to be ended, and he asked his father's permission to go to the University of Halle to study theology.

Schleiermacher himself did not understand this crisis, even at the time, to be a total loss of faith; he retained a belief in God, and his powerful sense of religious impulse, the 'piety' which he claimed, never left him. But from his father's point of view, one who had lost his faith in the divinity and atoning sacrifice of Christ could not be counted as a brother in Christ. Estrangement was inevitable.

At Halle, Schleiermacher's uncle, Professor Ernst Stubenrauch, took him into his house. No better arrangement could have been imagined. Professor Stubenrauch was a Professor of Reformed Theology, and as an 'enlightened' theologian he could well understand the pressures on his nephew. While the process of clearing out the 'rubbish of former ages' was going on,

Schleiermacher had the benefit of his self-effacing counsel and support. Schleiermacher took comparatively little notice of the theologians, immersing himself in the study of Kant and of the Greek classics. His reading was wide, and he felt himself uncommitted to any school. At the time he wrote to his father: 'Thus I quietly watch the combat of philosophical and theological athletes without proclaiming myself for any of them.'[7]

Throughout this period, Professor Stubenrauch had been unobtrusively acting as a mediator with Schleiermacher's father, and in 1790, when Schleiermacher, now 21, passed his first theological examination, the rift was substantially overcome. At the same time the problem of his future career remained unsolved, and Schleiermacher passed the next six years in considerable uncertainty. At first a tutor to a noble family, then, briefly, a teacher in a Berlin orphanage, he eventually took his second, qualifying theological examination (on his uncle's advice) and was ordained as an assistant to his uncle's brother-in-law, minister at Landsberg on the Warthe, an important town in Brandenberg (in modern Poland). This was in 1794, the year of his complete reconciliation with his father, just prior to his death. Only two years later, when his senior colleague died after a long illness and another man was appointed minister, Schleiermacher found himself again without employment. He was 27 years of age and the future did not hold out much promise.

First (Romantic) Period

A post was eventually offered as Reformed minister of the Charity Hospital in Berlin. It was not well-paid, and the congregation were humble people. If, however, he felt obliged to moderate the elevation of his language in his preaching, he more than compensated for this in the new circles of friends among

---

[7] quoted in F. W. Kantzenbach, *Friedrich Daniel Ernst Schleiermacher* (Rowohlt, 1967), p. 29.

whom he quickly made himself at home. At first he formed friendships in the circle of his ecclesiastical colleagues, J. J. Spalding (1714–1804) and F. S. G. Sack (1738–1817). Spalding was a leading theologian of the Enlightenment who had translated Butler's *Analogy of Religion* in 1756; and Sack was a family friend who had helped Schleiermacher for many years, and with whom he had co-operated in a German translation of some sermons of Hugh Blair (1717–1800), Regius Professor of Rhetoric in Edinburgh University. But Schleiermacher quite soon discovered more congenial companions in the younger, lay circles which were under the influence of the Classicism and Romanticism of Goethe and Herder.

The importance for Schleiermacher of this new flowering of social and intellectual contacts can scarcely be over-estimated; but it can at the same time be misjudged. It was not the case that Schleiermacher succumbed, as an unknown and lonely preacher, to the attractions of a worldly circle of sophisticates. It has often been forgotten that throughout this period he was preaching regularly to an ordinary congregation in the Hospital chapel; what is more, he took his duties with great seriousness. However, his new style of life was watched by Sack with understandable alarm, particularly when a close (but platonic) friendship grew up between Schleiermacher and the beautiful 32-year-old wife of one of the circle's leaders.

At this time also he met Friedrich Schlegel (1772–1829) who first arrived in Berlin in 1797. Though Schlegel was younger than Schleiermacher, he was already recognized as a leading figure of the Romantic movement. Schlegel's vision was nothing less than an attempt to unite science and art, poetry and philosophy, in one overall view of reality. A mutually enthusiastic friendship immediately sprang up between the two. Schlegel wrote to his brother that he hoped to learn a great deal from Schleiermacher, and Schleiermacher was deeply impressed with the breadth of Schlegel's interests. Schleiermacher, who was at the time engaged on translating into German more English sermons—those of Joseph Fawcett (1758–1804), a London dissenting minister and popular preacher—was quite probably persuaded by Schlegel to embark on something more adventurous, an address to his sophisticated friends on the subject of religion.

During the winter of 1798 and spring of 1799 the five speeches *On Religion*, 'speeches to the cultured among its despisers', were completed. With recent experience in mind Schleiermacher depicted his intended audience:

> But in our day especially, the self-styled life of cultured people hardly yields a glimpse of it [sc. religion]. You no longer visit the temples of religion. Indeed, I am aware that for you it is just as passé to worship deity in the quiet sanctity of your hearts. Setting out the clever maxims of our learned men and the resplendent lines of our poets as wall decorations will do very well—but, please, nothing more 'sanctimonious' than that! Suavity and sociability, art and learning, have won you over heart and soul—this no matter what little time or devotion you may give to them. These things dominate your lives so completely that no room is left for that eternal and holy being which, in your view, lies 'beyond this world.'[8]

The speeches, though not intended for delivery, were written in high-flown style of Romantic rhetoric and appeared anonymously. They were widely read, and ran through four editions (1799, 1806, 1821 and 1831), in which Schleiermacher made sometimes substantial alterations to eliminate misunderstandings. Reactions were diverse. While some of the great philosophers and literary figures commented favourably, Sack was horrified, and regarded the work as merely a brilliant apology for pantheism. This criticism (which has been frequently repeated over the years) did not deter Schleiermacher, since he was convinced it rested on a misunderstanding. From the reception accorded to the speeches *On Religion*, he felt encouraged to turn his attention to ethics. The result was the *Soliloquies* (German, *Monologen*), published, again anonymously, in 1800.[9] Here also Schleiermacher affected a lyrical style, which inhibited logical argument and struck even some of his contemporaries as artificial.

---

[8] *O.R.*, p. 39 (1).
[9] Translated by H. L. Friess (Open Court Publishing Co., 1926; reissued, also in paperback, 1957).

But the work, an exposition of the nature of individuality and of humanity, won him many more admirers and confirmed his position as a writer of singular power and promise.

Schleiermacher's life was now overshadowed by a personal problem which was to be with him until 1805. A close friendship sprang up between him and Eleonore Grunow, a married woman, whose marriage to an egotistic Berlin minister was childless and apparently loveless. Schleiermacher was quite clear that he could have married her and been very happy, and so long as she vacillated about a divorce he held out hope. He left Berlin in 1802 in order to bring her to a decision; but it was not until 1805 that she finally, from conscientious scruples, returned to her husband. His attitude towards the love of man and woman was romantic, in the sense that such love, he held, spiritualizes the absolutes of morality. In the precise circumstances of Eleonore's marriage he felt that divorce could be contemplated as stemming from a higher necessity than that of mere morality. This, too, alienated him from the orthodox of his time and later.

The removal from Berlin was a great personal blow. His new post, as Reformed minister to the castle court at Stolp in Pomerania (modern north-west Poland), involved preaching to tiny independent congregations, and led him later strongly to support the union of Lutheran and Reformed Churches in Prussia. He occupied himself, apart from preaching, with the great project, suggested by Friedrich Schlegel in 1798 and begun in 1800, of the translation of Plato's works into German. Originally Schlegel had planned to assist him; but in the event Schleiermacher undertook it almost entirely alone—an immense task, which was not completed until 1828.

In 1804, at the age of 35, he was released from his self-imposed exile by two offers of university posts, one in Würzburg and the second, which he took, in Halle. This latter was a dual appointment, with duties both as a lecturer and as University preacher. His academic work included Biblical exegesis, especially of Paul, and lectures in dogmatics, ethics and hermeneutics.

Schleiermacher's next publication, entitled *Christmas Eve*,[10] begins to show some of the fruit of his increasing attention to the problems of Christian doctrine. This book was cast in the form of a Platonic dialogue, in which a group of friends discuss the question of the meaning of the person of Christ. But the presence of a sceptic shows Schleiermacher's continued determination to keep the 'cultured among the detractors of religion' as partners in his presentation of Christian faith.

In 1806 Halle became involved in Napoleon's war against Prussia. On October 14 Napoleon won the battles of Jena and Anerstädt, and by October 27 he was in Berlin. The University of Halle was closed by his direct order. Despite this Schleiermacher stayed on for a year as preacher, living with his friend, the philosopher Henrik Steffens, in very meagre circumstances. After Halle had been assigned to the newly founded Kingdom of Westphalia under Napoleon's brother, Jérôme, Schleiermacher realized that it was time to leave. He went to Berlin and sought to occupy himself privately, both with lecturing and with political activity on behalf of the Prussian patriotic party. Schleiermacher had never been politically inactive; but from this point he was fully committed to the rescue of Prussia and the rebuilding of Germany under its lead.

Second (Main) Period

In 1808 Schleiermacher became engaged to the widow of a former friend and colleague, Ehrenfried von Willich. Von Willich had married in 1804 the sixteen-year-old daughter of an Army officer, and died only three years later, leaving her with one small child, and a second on the way. The young widow, whom Schleiermacher treated with great gentleness, leaned heavily upon him for support. Her gratefulness ripened into love, and they were married in 1809.

Thus opened a completely new period in Schleiermacher's

[10] Published 1805. Translated by T. N. Tice (John Knox Press, 1967).

life when he was 40. A new university had already been proposed in Berlin, in the construction of which he took a deep interest. In a short essay, *Occasional Thoughts about Universities in the German Sense* (1808) he argued strongly for the freedom and independence of universities from State control or influence, and for a liberal education in which each student would be compulsorily grounded in philosophical disciplines. Schleiermacher was co-opted into the education section of the Prussian Ministry of the Interior and worked on questions of curriculum.

In 1809, in the same month as his marriage, he became minister at Trinity Church. When the University opened in 1810, Schleiermacher was nominated Professor of Theology and first Dean of the Faculty. In 1811 he was honoured with the Fellowship of the Prussian Academy of Sciences. The new lectures he was now giving in the University led to new activity. In 1811 his *Brief Outline on the Study of Theology* appeared in print, and in the same year he prepared for the first time an introduction to philosophy, entitled *Dialectic*. This latter work, which can be reconstructed from Schleiermacher's lecture notes and those of students, he did not live to finish.

All this activity, including lectures on the history of philosophy and ethics, and on New Testament exegesis and dogmatics, was combined with an active political life. When, after long indecision, Frederick William III gave the command for the establishment of a voluntary army corps in 1813, Schleiermacher himself assisted with the recruiting. The defeat and exile of Napoleon in 1814 did not yield in Germany the measure of freedom and democracy that Schleiermacher, with many others, hoped for. When the Congress of Vienna (1814) set the old aristocratic order once more in the saddle, Schleiermacher became, with many of his colleagues in the University, politically suspect, and was removed from his post in the Ministry of the Interior. An episode in which Schleiermacher took the side of an imprisoned colleague led to open conflict with his colleague, the eminent philosopher, G. W. F. Hegel (1770–1831). In 1820 many Berliners were expecting him to be dismissed from his post, so unpopular had his stand against despotism of all kinds become among the ruling circles. Schleiermacher, however, was quite fearless, and to this fearlessness he owed his great popularity among the ordinary people of Berlin.

Schleiermacher was also active in the field of Church reform, particularly in encouraging lay participation in church administration. He warmly greeted the appeal of the King for a union between the Lutheran and Reformed Churches in Prussia, celebrating Holy Communion on the 300th anniversary of the Reformation (1817) together with a Lutheran colleague. These activities brought so much opposition from conservative churchmen and ecclesiastical politicians, that, when in 1821 the 3rd edition of his speeches *On Religion* was published, he felt that it would be more appropriate to address a new set of speeches 'to the hypocrites, to those in bondage to the dead letter, to the crass hardhearted dupes and fanatics'.[11] He felt deeply that Christianity was in danger of being identified with philistinism, and scientific method with infidelity.

The appearance in 1821/22 of Schleiermacher's main work in two volumes, *The Christian Faith*, did nothing to appease the opposition. Those who had already made up their mind on the basis of the speeches *On Religion* that Schleiermacher was a pantheist in disguise found nothing in *The Christian Faith* to make them revise their opinion. The freedom and effectiveness with which Schleiermacher both criticized the ecclesiastical creeds and formularies and sought a new way to base Protestant theology pleased none of the orthodox. Also the sceptics, who always prefer the old systems which they know how to refute to any new constructions, asserted that in reality Schleiermacher destroyed the Christian faith. David Friedrich Strauss claimed that the old rat's nest of traditional dogmatics was a greater value in its original stone and iron construction than the new, impermanently built garden house of *The Christian Faith*.

The Christian Faith had naturally also its enthusiastic admirers.

[11] O.R., p. 36 (from the Foreword to the third edition, not translated by Oman).

But Schleiermacher himself realized that he was unlikely to witness the full appreciation of his work. His next ten years were fully occupied with his liberal political endeavours, his work towards Church reform and further widening of his scope as lecturer into the fields of psychology and educational theory. Berlin University had grown in the period 1810–30 from 256 students (29 theologians) to 2488 students (641 theologians), the proportionally high development in the numbers of theologians being undoubtedly a tribute to the eminence of Schleiermacher.

In 1828 he made a private journey to England, staying in London and making trips to Windsor and Cambridge. Despite his having translated two works of British theology, he had no great love for Britain and his letters to his wife during his visit are not enthusiastic. Although he enjoyed his trip to Windsor and noted with approval, as a good democrat, that St Paul's contained monuments to ordinary young sea officers as well as to Nelson, he found the weather harmful to his health. He had already in the first edition of his speeches *On Religion* spoken very critically of Anglomania among his contemporaries, and against the 'miserable empiricism' which characterized the British approach to religion. Even in 1831 he felt unable to retract much from his earlier judgement.

A deep sadness overshadowed the last years of Schleiermacher's life, when in 1829 his only son and youngest child died. There were three older girls in the Schleiermacher family, in addition to his wife's two children by her former marriage.

In 1833 he travelled to Sweden and Denmark as a celebrity. An enthusiastic welcome awaited him in Copenhagen, where students greeted him with a torchlight procession. At Christmas of the same year he officiated at the marriage of his youngest daughter Hildegard. But the period of fame was to be short-lived. In February 1834 he contracted inflammation of the lungs, and died after an illness of only a week. During the funeral at Trinity Church the historian Ranke estimated that 20,000 to 30,000 mourners thronged the streets—proof of the esteem in which Schleiermacher was held by all, including his opponents.

One secret of his popularity was undoubtedly the breadth of his interests. Quite apart from the width of actual lectures, of his political, educational, and ecclesiastical commitments, and of his publications, he took part in learned societies of various kinds and interested himself in the history of art. He was also a great nature-lover and an indefatigable hiker. We have the impression of a man of great personal warmth who could be moved to tears by the deep seriousness of his own utterances in the pulpit, and who yet lived a life of joyous freedom. His formidable achievements in classical philological scholarship, Biblical exegesis, the study of the history and psychology of religions, political and ethical theory, and theological dogmatics, were grounded upon a living Christian faith and active member-ship of the Christian community. This was a basis not in the sense of a key which opened every door, or a set of facile assumptions which could be applied by ratiocination to every theoretical problem; but as a living ground of experience which informed, and was informed by, the provisional conclusions of all theoretical argument. Schleiermacher envisaged a constant two-way traffic between his religious and his intellectual life, and it is the measure of his greatness as a man that he was able so fully to embody his personal ideals in his creative life's work.

2

Thought

THE foregoing outline of Schleiermacher's life has divided his literary career into two periods, the romantic period (1796–1806), and the main period (1806–34). Dr Martin Redeker, the modern editor of Schleiermacher's *Christian Faith*, makes a similar division (though dating the main, systematic period from 1803, with Schleiermacher's entry into university teaching at Halle), and further divides the second period at 1811. At this time, he believes, a perceptible change takes place in Schleiermacher's attitudes, bringing him into a closer and more inward relationship with Christian doctrine and piety and altering some of his philosophical attitudes.[12] Whatever validity these attempts at division into periods may have, they are at least evidence for the difficulty of making a consistent interpretation of Schleiermacher's thought.

Even when we concentrate upon a very few of Schleiermacher's writings, as this essay does, the problem arises. It arises in the contrast, which has been often remarked upon, between Schleiermacher's two main books, *On Religion* and *The Christian Faith*. The contrast is, in the first instance, stylistic. The speeches *On Religion*, though never in fact delivered as speeches, are rhetorical throughout; they cajole, they satirize, they allude, they enthuse. *The Christian Faith*, on the other hand, aims at precision and exactitude. It is an ordered account of the content of Christianity, laid out in 172 paragraphs (the first edition of 1821/22 had 190), each expanded with explanation and

[12] M. Redeker, *Friedrich Schleiermacher* (Walter de Gruyter and Co., 1968), pp. 11 and 12.

development. Further, the intended readership of the two works can be contrasted. *On Religion* was designed for 'the cultured despisers'; *The Christian Faith*, which assumed the truth of Christianity, was clearly designed for Christian believers.

The problem which writers on Schleiermacher have to face is whether the two works, whose first production was separated by more than twenty years, represent two irreconcilable points of view. The actual gap of years can be closed somewhat by pointing to the fact that Schleiermacher went to considerable pains in the 'Explanations' or 'Supplementary Notes' appended to each speech in the third edition of 1821 to point out the fundamental consistency between the speeches and *The Christian Faith*. Further he had expressed his intention of publishing a handbook on Dogmatics as early as 1805, in connection with his first lectures on that subject in 1804/05 in the University of Halle. Despite this, it is perfectly possible for Schleiermacher to have embraced two ultimately contradictory premises in addressing two different sorts of audience. We have noted already that some of his contemporaries could not understand how, holding the views he expressed in *On Religion*, he could continue in his vocation as a preacher. To say that Schleiermacher himself felt no contradiction or even tension between the two standpoints, does not in fact settle the question.

The contrast, put at its crudest, is as follows: In the speeches *On Religion*, Schleiermacher appears to make Christianity of less importance than what he defines as *religion*. He very much wants his critics to become religious people; but does he really mind whether they become Christians? He says a great deal about how God is known, but very much less about Christ. In *The Christian Faith*, on the other hand, Christ becomes central. All consciousness of God is said to be mediated by Christ and the truth of the Christian faith is everywhere assumed.

This apparent contrast has given commentators on Schleiermacher much to worry about. Should what he says in the latter book be understood in the light of what he says in the former, or vice versa? The present writer is convinced that the contrasts are more a matter of style than of fundamental standpoint. He finds plenty of evidence of a basically consistent outlook, in which both development of views and divergences of emphasis must be allowed their natural place. The following exposition of Schleiermacher's thought, though itself divided into two parts concentrating separately on the two works, will be at some pains to emphasize their interrelatedness.

Doctrine of God

Schleiermacher was charged with teaching pantheism. There have been many variations on this critical theme, but one of the most literary is from the pen of the fine Scottish theologian, A. B. Bruce (1831–99). Speaking of the 'haze upon the page' of *The Christian Faith*, he says:

> You read the passage again with increasing attention, like one straining his eyes to see some object in moonlight, and still you fail to see the idea clearly. The reason is that it *is* moonlight through which you are looking —the moonlight of Christian faith reflected from the Christian conscious-ness of the writer upon the dark planet of a Pantheistic philosophy.[13]

Pantheism is difficult to define. If it means the theory that God and the universe are identical, then there is nothing to distinguish it from atheism. The great modern writer with a reputation for pantheism was B. Spinoza (1632–77), a Dutch Jewish philosopher, from whom Schleiermacher had certainly learnt much. But the idea of a personal God, such as that depicted in classical Christian theism, is on the face of it simply not compatible with a thorough-going pantheism. How then does Schleiermacher, a Christian theologian, come to be charged with having mixed his theology with this particular form of atheism?

It was the speeches *On Religion* which gave particular offence.

[13] *The Humiliation of Christ* (T. and T. Clark, 1876), pp. 206 f.

In 1801 Schleiermacher wrote a letter to F. S. G. Sack, in reply to his protest (see p. 9), and justified himself as follows:

> You say that I am a pantheist. Have I spoken of religion (in the sense in which you also take this word), have I spoken of faith in a personal God with scorn? Absolutely nowhere. I have only said that religion should not be dependent on whether one in abstract thought ascribes to the infinite, transcendental Cause of the world the predicate of personality. This is why I adduced Spinoza as an example, though I am so little like a Spinozist, because throughout his ethics there dominates that way of thinking which one can only call piety. I have pointed out that the reason why certain people ascribe personality to God while others do not lies in differing orientations of the mind, and at the same time I have shown that neither of them is a hindrance to religion.[14]

Schleiermacher's sensitivity to this charge is further shown by the heavy alterations to passages of the second speech which might be misunderstood; these alterations were carried out for the second edition of 1806, and (in the third edition of 1821) many of the 'Explanations' relate to the alleged pantheism of the work. *The Christian Faith* of 1830 also contains an important passage, where Schleiermacher asks whether pantheism, which he notes has never existed as an organized religion but has always been a nickname or a taunt, is compatible with piety.

> To this question an affirmative answer may be given without hesitation, provided that Pantheism is taken as expressing some variety or form of Theism, and that the word is not simply and solely a disguise for a materialistic negation of Theism.[15]

This makes it clear that the pantheism which Schleiermacher found valuable was not simply a negation of theism.

What then was it? The answer to this important question must be sought in the area of Schleiermacher's ideas about the relation of our knowledge of God to our knowledge and experience of our environment in the universe. Schleiermacher tries to overcome the, for him, crude dichotomy between the idea of God which presents him as working from outside the universe, and that which presents him as a force working through

[14] *Aus Schleiermachers Leben*, L. Jonas and W. Dilthey (ed.), III, p. 283.
[15] *C.F.*, p. 39.

the medium of the universe. But while he attempts to overcome this dichotomy in a whole new approach to the problem, some of his statements appear to exclude the external working of God. Schleiermacher's attitude to miracle illustrates this.

'Miracle' is simply the religious term for event. Every event, even the most ordinary and natural, is to be seen as a miracle as soon as it permits the religious view of it to become the predominant one. For me, therefore, everything is miraculous. For you what is inexplicable and strange is miraculous, but that is not what is meant by a miracle in my sense at all.[16]

The whole notion of the inexplicable as evidence for God must be abandoned. It is not in these peripheral areas that one meets with God, but in the very centre of life. In such passages the internal working of God through the medium of the universe is unquestionably emphasized, and some critics have concluded without further delay that Schleiermacher wishes to abandon the supernatural altogether.

The falsity of this conclusion must be allowed to emerge in the course of this section on Schleiermacher's doctrine of God. But we must notice from the start that Schleiermacher is not interested in presenting what he has to say about God, initially at least, in the form of a set of traditional propositions. The speeches *On Religion* contain very little directly about God; 'your God seems to me a little skinny', Friedrich Schlegel once remarked. But the speeches are in reality the groundwork for a Christian doctrine of God, which is presented indirectly in, one might say behind, a description of religion.

Why does Schleiermacher choose this indirect method of communication? There are two reasons, both of which are exceedingly important. In the first place, there are the precise circumstances of the speeches. He was addressing the 'cultured despisers' of religion, men who had succeeded in making their earthly life so rich and varied that they no longer stood in need of an eternity. These, however, were not, despite their name, really similar to contemporary sceptics. His chosen audience was society already influenced by the literary and philosophical

[16] *O.R.*, p. 141 (88). But see *C.F.*, pp. 71-73.

movement of German Idealism. In its programme, the uniting of science, art, and philosophy in an overall view of the world, Schleiermacher saw hope for a renewed understanding of religion. 'I gladly acclaim you to be the real, if unintentional, saviours and guardians of religion today.'[17] His method of appeal to them had, therefore, above all else to be couched in their language and to be dominated by their interests. The speeches *On Religion* are throughout apologetic and polemic. In particular the subject of religion is broached in the only way in which they would be able to understand it, namely by an act of self-awareness. The sensibilities, on which the Romantics prided themselves, were to be so purified in contemplation that the nature of religion would appear in its essence. They would then be in a position to realize, what Schleiermacher himself had realized, that religion, far from being a cramping and confining sacrifice of the intellect, gave the sole basis for a complete view of humanity and the world.

But quite apart from the necessity of communicating with men of his own day, there is a second, theological reason for the method of an indirect presentation of the doctrine of God. Schleiermacher wishes to reach behind the customary propositions about God—propositions relating to his being and his works, that he is love, creator of the world, omnipotent, and similar statements—to the experience of God which underlies them. This experience he terms 'religion' and he believes that there exists a qualitative difference between the propositions and the experience, which corresponds to the difference between coldness and warmth.

Thus by speaking of God indirectly, in a description of religion, he hopes to restore to theology what is lost when all that is presented is a neat set of propositions about God's attributes. The experience of God involves warmth, spontaneity and personal involvement. But the Enlightenment theology of Schleiermacher's day was (in his own words), 'the artifice of calculating intellect. . . . Here everything elapses into callous

[17] *O.R.,* p. 201 (141).

(*kalt*) argumentation. Here even the sublimest subjects are made pawns of controversy between competing schools of thought.'[18] Naturally in speaking of God words have to be used, and some attempt made, if not to describe religion with meticulous precision, then to compare it with something helpful. In fact Schleiermacher offers in the speeches *On Religion* a way of approaching the doctrine of God which he hopes will reflect the warmth of the original moment of religious experience.

At the same time Schleiermacher expressly recognizes the limitations of speech in the communication of religion. Words about religion, he admits, are the 'mere shadows of the inner stirrings of religion'.[19] And when he comes to consider the communication of religious feeling, he notes that it character-istically takes place in the context of friendship and love, where 'looks and gestures are clearer than words' and 'even solemn silences may be understood.'[20] The indirect method of speaking about God has the important advantage of calling attention to this aspect of religious language of which it is so easy to lose sight in more straightforward theology.

For both these reasons, the apologetic and the theological, Schleiermacher chose his indirect method; indeed the term 'God' had acquired for him all the wrong meanings. This is clearly illustrated in the closing passage of the second speech in its first form. There Schleiermacher baldly states, 'God is not everything in religion. He is only one thing and the Universe is more'.[21] In the second edition of 1806 this passage was altered to read, 'the usual conception of God as an individual being outside and beyond the world is not the whole story for religion. It is only one way of expressing what God is—a way, seldom entirely unalloyed and always inadequate'.[22] Schleiermacher

[18] *O.R.*, p. 55 (15).
[19] *O.R.*, p. 181 (122).
[20] *O.R.*, p. 211 (150).
[21] *Uber die Religion*, 1st edn. ed. by R. Otto (Vandenhoeck & Ruprecht, 1967), p. 99.
[22] *O.R.*, p. 156 (101).

shows here quite explicitly that he is intent on altering the usual conception of God to something more central to the daily experience of men.

In making this new attempt, Schleiermacher by no means abandons his position as a theologian speaking from an identifiably Christian standpoint. The evidence for this is the important role which the concept of 'mediation' plays from the start in his theology. In order to speak of God at all there must be those whose task is to interpret the ways of God to man. Part of their work is to bring order and unity into the world; among them are lawgivers and inventors, heroic figures and subduers of nature.[23] There are also those more spiritual, who strive 'to awaken the slumbering seed of a better humanity, to kindle love for higher things, to transform the commonplace into a nobler life, to reconcile the children of earth with heaven, and to counterbalance the heavy attachment of our age to things of crass value'.[24] Such men are the prophets and priests of humanity whose mission it is to mediate between the finite and the infinite.

It is no accident that this conception of the role of 'mediator' stands in the opening pages of Schleiermacher's appeal to his contemporaries. It corresponds closely both to the role of the genius in *Sturm und Drang* ideology, and to the programme of the unification of knowledge set by the Romantics as their own task. But in the hands of Schleiermacher it is given a distinctive emphasis. Throughout this first speech there are constant reminders both of the work of the prophets and also of the work of Christ. The phraseology of inspiration, mediation and reconciliation gives the unmistakable impression that the substance of this speech, behind the romantic terminology, is the self-revelation of God.

What concerns Schleiermacher above all is that this revelation is not understood by his contemporaries, who are misled into equating it with the dry systems of theology perpetrated by the Enlightenment theologians, or who reduce it to the sanction

[23] *O.R.*, p. 45 (6).
[24] *O.R.*, p. 46 (7).

required for the stability of the moral law. Of the latter reduction Schleiermacher is especially scornful. Throughout the speeches he regards as the greatest danger to religion that it should be used as a useful accompaniment to a moral life, and as a means whereby the conscience can be made a little sharper and more alert. 'Does religion descend from heaven for so meagre an end?' he asks. 'Hardly!'[25]

In the area of mediation, then, Schleiermacher is prepared to speak of the activity of God as being evident in certain particular individuals. Although he looks forward with the prophet Jeremiah to the day when humanity does not require such mediators, all being taught directly by God, he calls the rarity of such mediation a wise economy.[26] Such men, being so alone, feel themselves compelled to communicate what has been revealed to them in order that they may find companions. It is precisely this sense of compulsion which lies behind Schleiermacher's presentation of the speeches to his friends. 'To this pressure for communication I submit myself. Such is the very nature of my own calling.'[27] The claim that Schleiermacher makes for himself in these words is the prophetic and apostolic claim to speak with authority the word of the Lord. What he is offering is not merely a new theory, but also a testimony. He is therefore inviting his readers to judge the content of what he says, not merely on theoretical grounds, but by reference to his own individual life. It is at least a continuing problem, whether or not the verification of any religious statement does not in some degree involve this personal element.

At the same time Schleiermacher clearly recognizes the need to present not merely an individual personal experience, but some general conceptions which can be thought over and argued about. The structure of this conceptual grasp on the approach to the doctrine of God must now be presented.

(1) *The testimony to the being of God lies in man himself.* Therefore

---

[25] *O.R.*, p. 61 (21).
[26] *O.R.*, p. 47 (8).
[27] *O.R.*, p. 47 (8).

the being of God is known essentially in contemplation. 'Religion is essentially contemplative.'[28] In another place Schleiermacher calls the process of discovering religion a 'process of becoming inwardly perceptive by being-grasped-within-oneself (*Insichergriffensein*).'[29] But he does not equate religion with self-contemplation, any more than he equates God with the religious consciousness of man. But mystical self-contemplation remains for him the most appropriate road to the discovery of the essence of religion and he praises the 'divine' Plato and his followers for this feature of their writings.[30]

In commending the contemplative way to knowledge of God, Schleiermacher wishes to warn his readers against two prevalent misunderstandings of religion. These were that religion consisted either in assent to the theological propositions made about God or in the moral activities to which belief in him led. The essence of these misunderstandings is most simply explained in *The Christian Faith*. The attempts to express belief in God in the sphere of systematic knowledge or activity are attempts actively to grasp the being of God. By contrast, the way of contemplation expresses receptivity to being grasped by the being of God. This is the fundamental meaning of Schleiermacher's celebrated distinction, which has been so often misinterpreted, between feeling, knowing and doing. It is not the case that Schleiermacher withdraws religion from the areas of knowing and doing into a private world of pious feelings. He clearly states, in vain as far as some of his critics are concerned, that piety issues both in knowledge and activity.[31] He wishes to isolate, artificially and in contemplation alone, that 'moment' in which the individual is grasped by a reality over which he himself does not exercise control and which is present to him because it is given.

[28] O.R., p. 78 (36).
[29] O.R., p. 181 (122). This ambiguous word seems to imply the divine activity of 'grasping'. The whole passage was added in the third edition of 1821.
[30] O.R., p. 200 (139).
[31] C.F., pp. 8 f.

He distinguishes between the three spheres of feeling, knowing and doing in different ways. In *The Christian Faith* they are distinguished as above by reference to the activity or passivity involved. Feeling is abiding-in-self (*Insichbleiben*), whereas knowing and acting are a passing-beyond-self (*Aussichheraustreten*). The precise form of distinction is not, however, so important as the direction in which he wants to point those interested to making a judgement about religion and its validity. First, he says, on no account reduce it to morality. Second, do not attend primarily to the quasi-factual statements which men make about God, because God is not initially grasped as an object of knowledge in the sense that natural science or theoretical philosophy grasps its objects of knowledge. Attend rather to these moments when men are aware of being moved by God, since such awareness is 'the immediate consciousness of the universal being of all finite things in and through the infinite, of all temporal things in and through the eternal'.[32]

(2) *God is present for men in an awareness of the underlying unity of all individual experiences.* It is this principle which saves Schleiermacher's doctrine of God from being a private mystical experience. In the content of man's awareness of God is necessarily involved the understanding that he unifies for us all our ambivalent relationships with things and people. He gives purpose to our life in the sense in which we can understand it as continuous with nature and history. We can take into ourselves whatever we perceive, whoever we meet, and whatever happens to us, as perfectly harmonious with our own beings. God is himself this principle of harmony and unity. He is waiting, immanent; to be religious means to be open to Him and to perceive Him all about one.

> And so religion is indeed a life in the infinite nature of the whole, in the one and all, in God—a having and possessing of all in God and of God in all.[33]

[32] *O.R.*, p. 79 (36).
[33] *O.R.*, p. 79 (36).

Such consciousness of the unity of all things in the Infinite is contained in feeling. In a difficult but vital passage in the second speech, Schleiermacher attempts to describe how consciousness may be either determined as feeling (*Gefühl*) or as perception (*Anschauung*, Tice translates this as 'perspectivity') by encounter with the same object. The 'moment' of unity of perception and feeling has passed as soon as the consciousness reflects upon itself. But it is that 'moment' which is the 'moment' of revelation. In it the individual through his senses is identified with the Whole in the object. The recalling of this moment in feeling and in perception together comprises knowledge; the experience of the Whole in the object is recalled in feeling, which is the proper sphere of religion.[34]

Schleiermacher does not hesitate to include all feelings under the heading of piety.

> Your feeling is your piety, with two qualifications: first, in so far as that feeling expresses the being and life common to you and to the universe in the way described and, second, in so far as the particular moments of that feeling come to you as an operation of God within you mediated through the operation of the world upon you.[35]

There are no sensations which are not pious, except those which stem from disease. In an explanation added in 1821, Schleiermacher cannot resist ironically observing (against the celibacy of Roman clergy) that 'married love, and the whole natural process of sexual attraction involved in it, is not automatically and absolutely incompatible with a state of piety'.[36]

Both the speeches *On Religion* and the *Soliloquies* resound to the praise of love as the true spiritual climate of the knowledge of God.

> To receive the life of the World Spirit within oneself and thus to have religion, a man must first have discovered humanity, and this he can do only in love and through love. This is why humanity and religion are so

[34] O.R., pp. 84–90 (42–46).
[35] O.R., p. 89–90 (45).
[36] O.R., p. 161 (105).

intimately and inseparably conjoined. The longing for love, ever fulfilled and ever recurrent, brings one inevitably to religion.[37]

The most immediate form of contact with the Whole, Schleiermacher is saying, is not in the first instance through natural objects, but through other people. The first stage to appreciating the being of God as the Unifier of the world of our experiences is to discover humanity. It is only from the realization of being bound together with all, and of all being necessary, that a true individuality can be built. Only on the basis of an unaffectedly humble recognition of our one-sidedness, a deep contrition for our failings, and a desire for fellowship with others, can flourish a confident humanity and a joyful self-sufficiency. Schleiermacher compares the life of the individual to a single melodic line requiring the harmonic accompaniment of religion to produce its full effect.[38] Thus he affirms the place both of individuality and of corporate humanity in the midst of a doctrine of God, which appears on first sight to recommend mystical self-sinking in the All.

(3) *God is present for men in the awareness of having been placed here, here and now, in all our relationships, without our having willed it.* In the last section, God was depicted as the principle of unity; in this, He is the ground or Whence of everything. This awareness is what Schleiermacher calls the 'feeling of absolute dependence', the extolling of which, in Hegel's flippant phrase, makes a dog the most religious of beings.

Schleiermacher's understanding of this is again complex, but rewarding to grasp.[39] There is, says Schleiermacher, in every sensing consciousness an active and a passive element. When faced with an object the active element feels itself free in relation to the object, the passive element feels itself dependent in relation to the object. These feelings are relative to each, and are invariably combined with each other, though one may predomi-

---

[37] *O.R.*, p. 121 (72). The *Soliloquies* speak of love as the 'force of gravitation in the spiritual world' (p. 39).

[38] *O.R.*, p. 139 (87).

[39] See *C.F.*, pp. 12–26.

nate. Schleiermacher uses as an illustration the feeling of dependence which the citizen has when faced with the State. Although this is the dominant feeling, it may be combined (he speaks from experience) with a feeling of being able to exercise a directive or even counter-influence upon it, that is, a feeling of freedom.

At the same time, Schleiermacher says, the whole sensing self-consciousness can be conscious of itself being in a higher relationship of dependence upon Another, that is, of not itself having willed itself. This second relationship of dependence is described as absolute, since it is 'the consciousness that the whole of our spontaneous activity comes from a source outside ourselves'.[40]

The feeling of absolute dependence is never a pure feeling; it is always accompanied by feelings in the sensing self-consciousness. That is to say, it is always provoked by relationship to an object, and is accompanied in particular by sensations of pleasure or pain. This is what Schleiermacher means by his principle that religious experience is never a moment of pure awareness of God. To be aware of God means to be in relationship with an object and thus to be aware of other (relative) feelings, as well as a feeling of absolute dependence. An example which Schleiermacher offers is a feeling of suffering in the sensing self-conscious with which can be combined a feeling of trust in God in the higher self-consciousness. The two feelings may coexist, the one being not reducible to the other. From this example at least it is clear that there is no pantheistic identification of the world and God in Schleiermacher's doctrine of God.

What is set out above as Schleiermacher's doctrine of God is his *approach* to the doctrine of God, which may be seen in the speeches *On Religion* and the introductory sections of *The Christian Faith*. The divine attributes of eternity, omnipresence, omnipotence, omniscience, holiness, justice, mercy, love and wisdom, receive separate treatment in later sections of *The Christian Faith*, and it is not proposed to give an account of them here. It will be sufficient to note that Schleiermacher holds

[40] *C.F.*, p. 16.

that the right way of understanding these traditional propositions about God is to interpret them in the light of the religious
experiences which have given rise to them. The propositions
are not unimportant, but they do not have a speculative life of
their own apart from what Schleiermacher has sought to
establish as the basic way to approach the whole subject of
knowledge of God.

The Church and Christ

As we saw, Schleiermacher chooses from the start the standpoint of a mediator, a man with an irresistible urge to communicate the reality of his own vision of God's dealing with
men. For such a man only one standpoint is possible, that of his
own faith, in the context of religious community of which he is
a member. 'Religion must be social if it is to exist at all,' he
says. 'It is man's nature to be social. It is pre-eminently the
nature of religion to be so.'[41]

At the same time, it must be admitted that Schleiermacher's
references to the Church in the speeches *On Religion* are rather
half-hearted. While he is prepared to define and defend a
church as necessary to the promotion of real religion, he admits,
and joins in, the many popular complaints against its authori-
tarianism, its civil privileges and its numerous corruptions.
This is an entirely consistent feature of Schleiermacher's mature
theology. In the *Brief Outline*, he goes so far as to state the basic
principles of the discipline of theological 'polemics', whose task
is to develop an effective critique of the 'diseased deviations
arising in the community to which he [the theologian] belongs'.[42]
In the 'Explanations' added to the text of the speeches *On Religion*
in 1821, Schleiermacher acknowledges that his attack on the
Church as an institution was one-sided. In particular he admits
that he placed too low a value on the organization of the Church

[41] *O.R.*, p. 208 (148).
[42] *B.O.*, p. 31.

into a large institution, as compared with the local congregation springing into being in response to the needs of religious people.[43]

But Schleiermacher's consistent evaluation of the Church is in terms of the extent to which it fosters genuine fellowship and communion between its members. The necessity of the Church springs from the necessity of mutual communication between people in the same religious tradition. That the Christian Church, as a matter of historical fact, has frequently failed to promote such mutuality, is readily admitted. When speaking to critics who are primarily aware of the defects of the Christian Church Schleiermacher is content to urge:

> Allow yourselves to be conducted once again into the exalted community of religious souls. This fellowship is indeed scattered. It is almost invisible. Yet its spirit everywhere holds sway, even where only a few are gathered in the name of deity.[44]

For them, he considers that prime importance attaches to their participating in the life of that spirit, which is manifest in more than one community. But when addressing Christians, he can phrase his appeal more explicitly: Be what you are. The doctrine of the Church is that it is a communion inspired by the Holy Spirit and learning of Christ, in which every member is an essential part.[45] The need for mutual communication is established by the sheer content of the Christian doctrine of the Church. There is no discrepancy in attitude between the two types of appeal. Indeed a Christian who is convinced, as was Schleiermacher, that a great deal is defective in the visible Church has no alternative but to invite critics of it to look more widely than its narrow confines, if what the Church stands for is exemplified elsewhere.

The problem is not, however, confined to an evaluation of the Church. In the fifth speech *On Religion* Schleiermacher deals with 'the Religions'. It is this chapter which gives rise to the

[43] *O.R.*, p. 259 (197).
[44] *O.R.*, p. 242 (179).
[45] *C.F.*, p. 578.

suspicion that Schleiermacher equivocated on the question of the uniqueness of Christianity. For what is dealt with here is not merely 'the Church', but religion itself; here he appears to be using his understanding of religion as a means for sifting the religions. 'Now you are to discover religion in the religions'.[46]

According to Schleiermacher a 'positive' religion exists when one feature of the relationship between God and man has been elevated to a central position as expressing the *essential nature* of divine-human relations. A 'positive' religion is one which has its own identifiable form; and it receives its form from its account of how God and man are essentially related. This imparts both a distinctive atmosphere to that religion, and orientates all its many doctrinal elements towards one single centre. Both Judaism and Christianity are examples of positive religions, and were the nearest to hand for his readers. Judaism's account of the essential nature of divine-human relations centres upon 'direct and universal retribution'.[47] By this Schleiermacher means that everything in human experience, all growth, decay, fortune and misfortune, is interpreted as part of a great colloquy in word and deed between God and man. The question asked by the disciples of Christ, 'Who has sinned, this man or his parents?', is taken as a typical illustration of the essential tendency in Judaism to regard any event as a reward or punishment sent from God.

For Christianity it is otherwise. Here the essential, central understanding consists of the account of God's mediating and redemptive activity in response to the corruptibility and resistance of all finite existence. God mediates knowledge of himself and redeems man through signs and wonders and through his own ambassadors. We have already noted that Schleiermacher regarded his own ministry as mediatorial; here then is its proper meaning as an obedient response to the essential insight of Christianity. Whether Schleiermacher is right or wrong in claiming *this* to be the essential understanding of Christian faith

[46] *O.R.*, p. 274 (211).
[47] *O.R.*, p. 306 (239).

is irrelevant to the fact that he sees himself throughout as a Christian minister; and it is from this standpoint alone that he understands the positive religions. For the Christian faith treats other religions as material for its own distinctive religious standpoint.[48] Because its fundamental and characteristic understanding is that God is always seeking to redeem mankind, it is compelled to try to understand what God is saying to man through other religions. Built into Christian faith is the principle of receptivity.

This however does not mean that Christian faith has no *other* distinctive content. A considerable part of the fifth speech is devoted to rebutting the idea of a 'natural religion', a synthetic product which takes certain lowest common denominators of the religions and elevates them to the dignity of the 'natural' religion of man, i.e. what man would naturally believe if the priests and the enthusiasts left him alone. On the contrary, Schleiermacher argues that religion is naturally 'positive', that its essence is to have a definite form and characteristics. So-called 'natural religion', is parasitic on the existence of 'positive' religions; it is 'a faint echo' of the piety around it.[49] Not only is Schleiermacher hostile to 'natural religion', he firmly insists that Christianity 'because it expects to find godlessness . . . is polemical through and through'.[50] Its principle of receptivity is *not* a pretext for vague tolerance. 'Relentlessly Christianity . . . shows up every false morality, every poor religion, every unhappy mixing of morality and religion done for the sake of covering their nakedness.'[51] Its receptivity to other religions is based on its convictions about man's natural condition and the redeeming will of God.

Schleiermacher's account of the person of Christ is consistent with this standpoint, though in the speeches *On Religion* it is clearly less than adequate. The reason for the inadequacy was

[48] *O.R.*, p. 310 (242).
[49] *O.R.*, 299 (233).
[50] *O.R.*, p. 310 (242).
[51] *O.R.*, pp. 310 (242–43).

the pressure of space, and in the subsequently added 'Explanations', he pleads in more than one place to be understood in the light of what he wrote elsewhere. Christ, in Schleiermacher's fifth speech, is primarily the teacher of the characteristic idea of mediation, and being so is himself the bearer of that mediation. Relying here, as elsewhere later, explicitly upon the gospel of John as conveying the authentic tradition of the teaching of Jesus, he asserts that Jesus possessed a unique knowledge of God. This unique knowledge, together with his power to convey it to others and to draw them into its circle, is what is referred to when Jesus is spoken of as the mediator, or as divine. Jesus never denied that others might also be mediators; indeed, he insisted that all his disciples should themselves attempt to mediate knowledge of God through Christ. Nor did he restrict religious truth to what he himself taught, as though others from the same basic perspective might not further develop that teaching. The unity of the self-revelation of God, recognized by the criterion of Christ's own mediatorial ministry, is a fundamental teaching of Christianity.

At this point we leave the exposition of the speeches *On Religion* for the much fuller development of the same themes in *The Christian Faith*. In doing so, however, we are bound to remark that, at several crucial points in the section on Christ in the fifth speech, various additions and explanations in the later editions indicate obliquely the kind of misunderstanding to which Schleiermacher had exposed himself in his writing. In the first edition he had roundly declared that anyone who takes what he had defined as the essential Christian perspective as the basis for his religion is a Christian, whether or not he is a member of any Christian denomination. In later editions he has to add the remark that such a person will naturally acknowledge Christ 'when he is shown the whole meaning of Christ's coming'.[52] Schleiermacher does not allow that he has changed his view; he is merely correcting a one-sided statement. For him, Christ is

[52] *O.R.*, p. 317 (248).

the centre of all mediation.[53] But it may also be said that other revelations of God, consistent with his self-revelation in Christ, occur *outside* Christianity. Only it is emphasized more strongly in the later work that it is the destiny of all other faiths to pass into the Christian Faith, which alone mediates consciousness of God in a final and unsurpassable manner.

We pass therefore to consider the maturer exposition of Christology which Schleiermacher was able to give in his *Christian Faith*.

(1) *The Christian Church is an educational community in which is conveyed not merely a message, but Christ himself.* We are bound to start with the importance for Schleiermacher of understanding communication aright. For Christ's own preaching was a self-communication, and it is of the essence of the Church's activity to strive to realize that perfection. Schleiermacher pays, therefore, particular attention to types of speech in which the Christian Church communicates. He differentiates between poetic, rhetorical and didactic modes of speech, each of which informs and enriches the others.[54]

Theology, which is Schleiermacher's task in *The Christian Faith*, aims at a didactic mode of speech, free from the apparent contradictions of poetic and rhetorical speech. While it sets itself the ideal of that normative degree of definiteness which characterized Christ's own self-proclamation, it recognizes that self-proclamation can only very rarely supply the phraseology of its writing. Nor is doing theology a matter of making logical deductions from Christ's recorded statements. The task is more complex than even that might be. For what is being communicated is not mathematical propositions, but the truth about God. Thus all that Schleiermacher had argued for in his speeches *On Religion* is directly relevant to his laying out of belief in Christ and its communication. Speaking about Christ must have the character of bearing testimony to what Christ had done in and

[53] O.R., pp. 333–34 (263–64).
[54] For all this see *C.F.*, pp. 76–83.

for oneself; to speak of Christ is to speak of what one knows of redemption.

This is the method which Schleiermacher imposes upon the whole structure of his dogmatic theology. He divides his work into two parts. The first part elucidates what the concept of redemption presupposes, for example, what it means to be aware of being dependent upon God. And the second part describes the working out of the Christian's redemption in his consciousness of sin and grace. The first part takes the subjects of creation and the attributes of God in relation to the world; and the second, the doctrines of sin, of Christ, of the Church and of the last things. But, from first to last, Schleiermacher's aim is to bring out the way in which everything which claims with justice to be part of Christian theology must be clearly part of the Christian experience of redemption. Nor is it sufficient to show that every part of theology has a formal or logical connection with redemption; it must correspond (and bear witness) to some genuine inner awareness or consciousness of God on the part of the contemporary Christian believer.

Schleiermacher faces, of course, a still harder task in *The Christian Faith* than in his speeches *On Religion*, where his chosen rhetorical style lent itself to that 'warmth' of language which he felt that recent orthodox theology had lacked. In *The Christian Faith* he has to attempt to capture that warmth in still more precise phraseology. Stylistically his work is complex, and even his modern German editor remarks on the difficulty of understanding the involved periods of his sentences.[55] But it is not a matter of style, so much as of method, which is Schleiermacher's main difficulty. Does he succeed in his stated aim of making his doctrinal statements correspond to the inner awareness of the Christian?

Modern hostile commentators have been so much perturbed by the novelty of Schleiermacher's theological method, that they have scarcely paused to ask whether Schleiermacher is successful

[55] Martin Redeker (ed.), *Der Christliche Glaube* (Walter de Gruyter & Co., 1960) I, p. xli.

by his own standards. Indeed the question is a personally searching one, since it requires some exposure of the Christian's own experience. But the most impressive factual testimony to the success of Schleiermacher is the interest in his writings so many years later. He would himself have found this interest puzzling, since it was his view that Christian dogmatics attempted to systematize the doctrine prevalent in a Christian Church at a given time.[56] That churchmen should read his work with real profit over a century later suggests strongly that Schleiermacher's concerns are central to the theological enterprise.

(2) *Ecclesiastical formulae concerning the person of Christ need to be subjected to continual criticism.*[57] Schleiermacher's chosen method makes him critical, not merely of the lack of warmth in so much of the theology of his day, but also of the traditional content of that theology. Damage had been done to the Christian faith, he felt, when a purely speculative interest had come to dominate the formation of doctrine. 'Dogmatic propositions never make their original appearance except in trains of thought which have received their impulse from religious moods of mind'.[58] The important word here is *impulse*. Schleiermacher was by no means averse to the systematic organization of doctrine, which he unhesitatingly described as a positively 'scientific' (*wissenschaftlich*) activity. But the *impulse* to make doctrinal statements springs from a 'religious mood of mind', or, as we might say, a devotional mentality. This impulse is lost when the interest in the topic becomes a purely scientific or disinterested one, and when no connection exists between what is asserted as theological truth and the actual religious experience of the believer. Schleiermacher's attitude is, however, very far from being anti-intellectual. He had to contend all his life with those Christians who were not prepared to give any thought to their faith.

To abbreviate the above discussion one might say that Schleiermacher felt free to criticize *dogma* in the name of *religion*.

[56] *C.F.*, p. 88.
[57] *C.F.*, p. 389, para. 95.
[58] *C.F.*, p. 82.

And no better or more important example exists of his critical activity than the way he treats traditional Christology. The traditional doctrine is that there are two natures, divine and human, inseparably united in the one person of Christ. With the intention of asserting the existence of God in Christ and of Christ's corporate fellowship with humanity, Schleiermacher is unhesitatingly in agreement. But he strongly objects to the traditional way of expressing it. For he maintains that in ordinary usage it is intolerable for one person to have two quite different natures, which would preclude any real unity of life. Also, attempts to explain the unity in duality of the life of Christ rarely achieve anything other than 'a demonstration of the possibility of a formula made up by combining indications out of which it is impossible to construct a figure'.[59] Since the basic formula contains this apparent contradiction, it could only be defended in a whole series of negative attempts to prove that no contradiction resulted. Thus theology ceased to be of any use to religious life; and Schleiermacher points out that even the most orthodox theologians in their devotional writings scarcely anywhere use the formal dogmatic terminology.

The criticism which Schleiermacher levels against traditional Christological language is far-reaching. For as a matter of fact, theology had used that language as a guide, if only a verbal one, to ensure orthodoxy. To reject it freed the theologian from the necessity not only of using the terminology, but also of attempting to show that alternative terminology was in fact in agreement with it. But to what criteria of orthodoxy is Schleiermacher then bound? In what way does he regulate his reconstruction of Christology? His answer marks a turning point in the history of Christian doctrine; he starts from a definition of the *essence of Christianity* and holds his Christology to agreement with it. We should notice that having rejected traditional ecclesiastical usage, he does not now turn to Scriptural usage. Instead he offers as a guide his own intuition of the basic nature of Christianity, a faith in which everything is related to the

[59] *C.F.,* p. 393.

redemption wrought for man by Jesus Christ. For this to be true, man must be both in need of redemption and capable of receiving it; and Christ must be capable of imparting redemption to man. His understanding of Christ must therefore show that he is distinctively superior to all men, and also that he is essentially like all men. The theologian must avoid, in other words, the traditional Christological heresies of ebionitism and docetism. The fact that avoidance of these two heresies has been the main concern of traditional ecclesiastical Christology encourages Schleiermacher to believe that his definition of the essence of Christianity is a faithful representation of Christianity's true nature.

Thus although Schleiermacher's substitution of a definition of the essence of Christianity for ecclesiastical or Scriptural authority is a turning-point in theology, he does not by any manner of means intend any radical departure from Christian tradition. His constructive Christology is argued for both from traditional credal statements and from the Biblical testimony. But then, true to his method, he is prepared to hold a critical question mark against those elements of Biblical testimony which he considers in no way to bear upon his definition of the essence of Christianity. For example, he is quite prepared to be critical of the doctrine of the Virgin Birth, and to allow that one might believe in Christ as redeemer without believing in his supernatural conception without male activity. Schleiermacher is quite clear, however, that the existence of Christ as Redeemer is only adequately represented when he is said to have been super-naturally conceived, in a way which altered maternal (and paternal) influence and removed all ground for human sinfulness.

Remarkably enough, Schleiermacher is critical also of the stories of the resurrection and ascension. Believing (on Biblical evidence) that the disciples recognized Christ as Son of God before the resurrection, he sees no reason to ground the efficacy of the redemption wrought by Christ upon such alleged facts. Neither his spiritual presence, nor his continued influence, is established by either story. He believes that a sober historical judgement must be passed on the stories; 'all that can be required of any Protestant Christian is that he shall believe them in so far as they seem to him to be adequately attested'.[60] Schleiermacher does not for a moment doubt the personal survival of Christ, nor that the Christian's belief in the survival of death rests upon Christ's *teaching* about such survival. But he feels able, at the same time, to be critical of the stories of a visible resurrection and ascension, which he does not regard as necessary to believing that Christ was raised in glory 'to the right hand of the Father'.

(3) *Christ redeems man by the power of his consciousness of God.* The reconstruction of the account of belief in Christ springs directly out of Schleiermacher's concern for an interest in man's awareness of God, which we examined in the section on the doctrine of God. But whereas in the speeches *On Religion* comparatively little attention is given to that which hinders awareness of God, though it is certainly mentioned, in *The Christian Faith* a much stronger account emerges of the phenomenon of alienation from God and of consciousness of sin. Schleiermacher urges that, from the first, man was both originally perfect and yet also originally sinful. By man's perfection he understands an original and still universal predisposition towards consciousness of God, and the ability to communicate such consciousness in fellowship with other men.[61] And by man's sinfulness, he understands a natural incapacity for good arising from man's fleshly existence, and the universal experience of the fact that the flesh is a powerful reality long before the potentialities of one's spiritual consciousness have developed. The condition of original sinfulness guarantees that man's consciousness of God is everywhere vitiated, and that man's spiritual life tends to be dominated by the flesh. Such is the human condition that redemption by Christ reveals.

For Christ himself is 'free from everything by which the rise

---

[60] *C.F.*, p. 420.
[61] *C.F.*, pp. 244 ff.

of sin in the individual is conditioned'.[62] He is thus something new in history, a special result of divine creative activity, both unparalleled and ideal. The cancelling out of the normal inheritance of sinfulness was a supernatural act, though, as we saw, Schleiermacher feels that the Virgin Birth narrative does not in any way guarantee the supernatural element. By reason of this freedom from the inheritance of sin, Christ's God-consciousness developed from earliest childhood as an undisturbed relationship to and knowledge of God. And this absolutely powerful God-consciousness, which Schleiermacher speaks of as a higher God-consciousness, is what is referred to as the existence of God in Christ, or the 'divine nature'. Our lesser and lower consciousness of God cannot, however, be termed an existence of God in us, except in so far as we relate it to Christ.

Thus Schleiermacher has a conception of Christ as organically human and like all men in virtue of this humanity; yet wholly superior to humanity in possessing an unclouded awareness of God. He is able to become the Redeemer of men, both by sharing the common condition of humanity and by assuming men into the power of his consciousness of God, thus freeing them from bondage to lower influences. Schleiermacher speaks of the attractive power of Christ and of his educative influence as a continuation of the divine, creative and person-forming activity which was the origin of the person of Christ.[63] When an individual is attracted by the person and teaching of Christ, he is drawn into a vital and living fellowship with him, which both evokes a consciousness of sin and conveys the power to overcome it. Schleiermacher speaks of his view of this fellowship with Christ as a mystical one, and differentiates it both from a purely empirical one (as the relationship between teacher and disciple), or from a magical one (as a transaction between Christ and God, imparted to man). The truth of his view, he believes, is established by the experience of the Christian believer.

[62] C.F., p. 383.
[63] C.F., pp. 425 ff.

Much more, of course, remains to be said about Schleiermacher's development and elucidation of these themes, as well as his penetrating criticisms of earlier views. In particular, Schleiermacher has a great deal to say about the fellowship of Christians, about the Holy Spirit and the new corporate life of the Church. In these doctrines his concern for the social character of all religion emerges to counterbalance the possible individualism of the emphasis upon experience. But enough has been said to indicate the character of Schleiermacher's reconstruction of Christology. From the standpoint of the contemporary Christian the redeeming activity of Christ consists in the power for freedom from our sensuous natures which exists in the attracting and compelling portrait of Christ as communicated in his Church.

The Christian Faith was an organization of the content of theology for the purposes of the contemporary Christian. But the system is not as self-enclosed as it perhaps sounds. Schleiermacher's method keeps open the problem of the relation of faith in Christ to the universal consciousness of God. His view is that Christ in fact himself mediates all consciousness of God. Our darkened and imperfect God-consciousness is an existence of God in human nature 'only in so far as we bring Christ with us in thought and relate it to Him'.[64] This is fundamentally consistent with his contention in the later editions of the speeches *On Religion* that Christ is the centre of all mediation.[65]

Does then the universal consciousness of God, of which Schleiermacher speaks, play no part in the assessment of the significance of religions other than Christianity or, indeed, of the pious disposition which embraces no particular religion or holds to heterodox doctrines? It is certainly the case that the existence of a universal original consciousness of God is not the grounds for an optimistic evaluation of the future of humanity. Although Schleiermacher speaks of original perfection, apart from the redeeming activity of Christ he holds out little hope for

64 *C.F.*, p. 387.
65 *O.R.*, pp. 333-34 (263-64).

human progress or the conquest of spirit over flesh. At the same time, Schleiermacher finds it unsatisfactory to suppose that a whole section of humanity is lost irretrievably, or perishing without knowledge of Christ. Hence he postulates, as a corollary of the divine creative activity in the person of Christ, a universal redemption of all souls, each when his time is fully come. His method demands that this be justified by reference to a Christian religious emotion; it is said, therefore, to be contrary to Christian sympathy that part of the human race should be entirely excluded from redemption.[66]

[66] *C.F.,* pp. 539 ff.

3

Significance

SCHLEIERMACHER knew from the outset that he was not going to please many of his clerical contemporaries. Already in the first edition of the speeches *On Religion* he predicted that his writing was not like anything that his fellow ministers would gladly hear.[67] And twenty years later he felt constrained to write that his experiences with his colleagues merely confirmed the judgement that any 'deeper penetration into the essence of religion generally and a genuinely accurate and historical way of perceiving the present situation of religious practice are much too rare among members of the clergy'.[68] Schleiermacher's conservative opponents assailed him in kind. But for 100 years Schleiermacher's achievements effectively dominated the German Protestant theological scene. He dominated not in the sense that all subsequent writers follow him, which is not even remotely the case; but in the sense that he had put his finger on *the* problem for any modern liberal theology, that of trying to produce some criterion by which true and false in traditional Christian theology might be discovered.

It is in this sense that Schleiermacher is the father of modern theology. Schleiermacher is the first great figure to turn his mind to the problem of the future development of theology in the modern environment. And his broad basic education and subsequent range of interests ensure the fact that his wrestling with this problem is deep and subtle. Even if theological research and debate has greatly progressed since his time, and

[67] *O.R.*, p. 41 (3).
[68] *O.R.*, p. 62 (22).

even if it were true that he committed grave errors in terms of his own time, it would still be the case that we could profitably learn from his work.

But it is also true that, particularly in the last 50 years, it has come to be widely asserted and believed that, for all his greatness, Schleiermacher is responsible for having put theology on the wrong track. The reason behind this belief takes us back to 1914 when 93 German intellectuals, among them a substantial number of liberal theologians, signed a manifesto supporting the war policy of the Kaiser. Just before this date Schleiermacher's reputation had risen to a peak of respect as liberal Protestant scholarship carried forward his programme of theological and historical enquiry. In 1914 at least one theologian of great future significance came to believe that the liberal theology of the nineteenth century had no future. That man was Karl Barth (1886–1968). In 1922 he was saying:

> With all due respect to the genius shown in his work, I can *not* consider Schleiermacher a good teacher in the realm of theology because, so far as I can see, he is disastrously dim-sighted in regard to the fact that man as man is not only in *need* but beyond all hope of saving himself; that the whole of so-called religion, and not least the Christian religion, *shares* in this need; and that one can *not* speak of God simply by speaking of man in a loud voice.[69]

Two years later he was praising the book of a colleague, Emil Brunner (b. 1889), for being really free of Schleiermacher's premises. There is much to be said for the view that Barth's own massive contribution to theology was to some degree explicitly designed as an attempt to obliterate Schleiermacher by a corresponding counter-achievement.[70]

The significance of Barth's opposition to Schleiermacher is very considerable. Although Barth himself indicated in a fascinating autobiographical essay at the very end of his life that his relationship to Schleiermacher's work was deeply ambivalent

---

[69] *The Word of God and the Word of Man* (Harper Torchbook, 1957), pp. 195 f.

[70] K. Barth, *From Rousseau to Ritschl* (S.C.M. Press, 1959), p. 308.

and ultimately unresolved,[71] his early hostility influenced many theologians in the 1930s and 40s. For example, H. R. Mackintosh's influential work, *Types of Modern Theology*, first published in 1937, is in many places markedly Barthian in its criticism of Schleiermacher. In reaction to Schleiermacher's prophecy that his apparently heterodox doctrine of God would soon enough come to be regarded as orthodox, Mackintosh firmly retorts, 'No prophecy could have gone wider of the truth'.[72] Such confidence might have been justified in 1937; but today, after some experience of Paul Tillich speaking of God as 'Ultimate Concern', we may rightly point to a returning swing of the pendulum. It has thus become possible comparatively recently to free ourselves from some of the unfavourable impressions made by critics under Barthian influences and to consider again the significance of Schleiermacher's work for modern theology.

Doctrine of God

There exist obvious resemblances between Schleiermacher's approach to knowledge of God through our sense of dependence upon the Whence of things and theologies which speak of 'Ultimate Concern' and 'Ground of our being'. Tillich indeed explicitly acknowledges his debt to Schleiermacher's discussions of theological issues. But the question which immediately occurs to the Christian reader is whether all this new terminology is in fact about the God and Father of our Lord Jesus Christ, and if so whether it is strictly necessary.

To answer this takes us at once to the heart of the most important problem for theology today, the issue of religious language. Schleiermacher helpfully emphasizes that there is more than one mode of speech in religion. To speak of God as the Whence of things is not an alternative to speaking of him as

[71] in *Schleiermacher-Auswahl*, ed. by Heinz Bolli (Siebenstern Taschenbuch Verlag, 1968), pp. 290–312.
[72] *op. cit.*, p. 83.

God and Father of our Lord Jesus Christ. To understand what is meant to be communicated by the words, we have to attend to the context in which they are uttered. Thus a strictly theological context must be differentiated from a liturgical context and the language used is not of the same type.

In the strictly theological context in which Schleiermacher wishes to employ his 'Whence of things' language, he is attempting to root his language about God in some specific state of affairs. This state of affairs is the alleged existence of religious experience, and Schleiermacher's attempt is of lasting significance to our own day. For if the word God is to be used at all in our language, it has somehow to be distinguished in content from a nonsensical word; and it can only be distinguished satisfactorily if something can be said about it which anchors it to some specific state of affairs. In pre-Enlightenment times this problem did not appear to be pressing because the theologian always was able to point in the end to the authority of Bible and Church as the places where God made himself known. But for a liberal theology which acknowledges that it is possible to disbelieve what both Bible and Church teach, the question of why one should believe in God becomes inescapable in its own terms. Something has to be pointed to as evidence; and Schleiermacher begins a whole tradition of theology by pointing to human religious experience.

Religion

But what of those who do not have, or say that they do not have, any such experience? This question became inescapable when posed by Dietrich Bonhoeffer (1906–45), who was at one time a disciple of Barth's. In his posthumously published *Letters and Papers from Prison* he assailed the idea that what he called the 'religious *a priori*', a sense of inwardness, is necessarily a permanent feature of human consciousness, and advanced the thesis that we are moving to a 'completely religionless time'.[73] If this is really the case, then Schleiermacher's whole attempt to base his theology on a contemplative religious awareness is due to be abandoned. Bonhoeffer wrote his letters in 1943–45, but they were not published until 1951 (in German) and 1953 (in English). They helped to prompt an immense literature on the subjects of religionless Christianity, the secularization of religion and, eventually, the 'death' of God. Much of this concentrates on the extent to which the knowledge and culture of the modern western world have made either difficult or impossible the religious assumptions of less secular times.

But is this in fact true? Or if it is true, is it to be tolerated? The value of Schleiermacher is that he recalls us to the phenomenon of religion not merely in its western context, but as a whole human phenomenology of religion, pursued subsequently by Rudolf Otto (1869–1937), an ardent admirer of Schleiermacher, and Edmund Husserl (1859–1938). Although such a discipline may not be able to establish the validity of religious experience as an autonomous aspect of human life, it serves to remind us of the deep-rooted subtlety of the diverse forms of such experience. This reminder will be of considerable value as an antidote to the sweeping generalizations about 'religion', which have stemmed from writers under the influence of Bonhoeffer.

In particular, the position of importance which Schleiermacher's exposition of religions gives religions other than Christianity is a valuable feature of his work. The theologian's task, says Schleiermacher in the *Brief Outline,* is 'to endeavour both to understand the essence of Christianity in contradistinction to other churches and other kinds of faith, and to understand the nature of piety and of religious communities in relation to all other activities of the human spirit'.[74] This twofold task involves a double obligation, to one's fellow Christians and to humanity. There have been those who have charged Schleiermacher with not fulfilling one or other of these obligations; but the essential

[73] *op. cit.,* (S.C.M. Press, 1967), p. 152.
[74] *B.O.,* p. 24.

sanity of Schleiermacher's approach survives the criticisms. It is a fact of some significance for theology today that he sought to preserve a balance between that which divides Christian faith from other faiths and that which draws the Christian in a receptive frame of mind towards other faiths. A task which certainly still confronts Christian theology is that of understanding the nature of the dialogue of religions into which the Christian feels drawn; indeed, which is largely of his own creating.

A Prince of the Church

In the *Brief Outline*, Schleiermacher defines a prince of the Church as one in whom 'both a religious interest and a scientific spirit [is] conjoined in the highest degree and with the finest balance for the purpose of theoretical and practical activity alike'.[75] Comparatively few theologians of the nineteenth or twentieth centuries have anything like the formidable academic achievements of Schleiermacher to their credit. But even when full justice has been done to these, there remains something important to be said both about Schleiermacher's practical activities and his 'piety' (to use his own word). As a political figure, and as a churchman, he did not hesitate to make costly stands about freedom and toleration, at a time when those were far from popular in official circles. His devotion to the cause of a Prussian revival was by no means an uncritical nationalism; even Barth is prepared to believe that he would not have signed the manifesto of 1914![76]

Of Schleiermacher's piety it is more difficult to write objectively. The tradition of contemplation which Schleiermacher seeks to perpetuate in Christian theology is exceedingly ancient. When Augustine speaks of the 'pleasures of the soul' in reference to the Psalmist's words, 'With the torrents of thy pleasures Thou wilt give them to drink', he expects to be understood only by a

75 p. 21.
76 *Schleiermacher-Auswahl*, pp. 293 f.

man who yearns, who is hungry and thirsty and who 'sighs for the Eternal country'.[77] Only such a man, Augustine believes, will understand what he is saying; but a cold man will think it nonsense. The aesthetic themes in Christianity are not accidental or disposable features of it, any more than are its moral themes; and it is greatly to Schleiermacher's credit that he attempted to hold them together.[78]

Schleiermacher was clearly a man who strongly felt the pull of the Eternal country upon his mind. I believe that it is misleading to speak pejoratively of this aspect of Schleiermacher's thought as 'pietism'. That his family and educational background brought him into contact with pietistic circles and that he regarded himself as being in some sense faithful to his origins is undeniable. But we need another, less emotionally loaded term to describe those important elements of continuity which he never wavers, even when harshly criticizing the revival of pietism in the 1820s.[79] I propose the term 'Platonist', to describe that deep urge for an intuitive vision of the wholeness of life which has warmly responded to the 'mysticism' of Paul and John throughout the Christian centuries.

It is this 'Platonism' which, I believe, makes Schleiermacher's theology of immediate appeal, provided we also bear in mind the attraction of its critical vigour and balance. Christian theology has been so deeply influenced by Platonism, from the third century to go no further back into history, that its relationship to it has become almost instinctive; it 'feels' right when set out in this way. Schleiermacher's theological achievement was exactly that; to set out a modern, critical theology in fundamentally 'Platonist' terms and in such a way that we 'feel' at home with it. Consistent with this is the recurrent appeal to the Gospel of John and to those claims for intuitive knowledge of God which are found in both John and Paul.

[77] *Tractate on John* 26, 4, translated by P. Brown in *Augustine of Hippo* (Faber, 1967), p. 375.

[78] See especially *Soliloquies* III.

[79] *O.R.*, p. 205 (144–45).

One example of Schleiermacher's attitude, which particularly endears him to the modern mind, is his scornful polemic against the 'theologians of the dead letter'. He will have nothing to do with 'that dogmatizing love of system' which 'obstructs truly vital knowledge of God, as much as may be within its power, and turns living doctrine into the dead letter'.[80] And yet, powerful though this attack is, it is balanced by an attack on those who have a distaste for polemics, 'who plaster the label "dead letter" on everything that is distinctively different', and who maintain an attitude of shallow indifference![81]

Schleiermacher's instinctive appreciation of the great variety of doctrinal interpretations corresponding to the variety of living experience did not in the end blind him to the necessity for a firm and positive content to Christian doctrine. 'The dead letter' was the death of that warmth and personal response to Christian doctrine which he himself felt and which he wished to convey by some means in his theology. But it was no slogan behind which to hide a slothful indifference to truth; and his contemporary appeal consists largely in the fact that he himself exhibited the balance of 'religious interest and scientific spirit' of the true prince of the Church.

[80] O.R., p. 166 (110).
[81] O.R., pp. 304–05 (238).

Principal Works by Friedrich Schleiermacher Available in English

in order of composition

On Religion: Speeches to its Cultured Despisers, London (Routledge, & Kegan Paul), 1893. Reissued, New York (Harper Torchbook), 1958. A new translation and critical edition by T. N. Tice, Richmond, Virginia (John Knox Press), 1969.

Soliloquies, Chicago (Open Court Publishing Co.), 1926. Reissued, also in paperback, 1957.

Christmas Eve: A Dialogue on the Celebration of Christmas, Edinburgh (T. & T. Clark), 1889. A new translation, Richmond, Virginia (John Knox Press), 1967.

Brief Outline of the Study of Theology, Edinburgh (T. & T. Clark), 1850. New translation entitled *Brief Outline on the Study of Theology*, Richmond, Virginia (John Knox Press), 1966.

The Christian Faith, Edinburgh (T. & T. Clark), 1928. New York (Harper Torchbook), 2 vols., 1963.

Also published as selections from Schleiermacher:

The Life of Schleiermacher as Unfolded in his Autobiography and Letters, London (Smith & Elder) 2 vols., 1860.

Selected Sermons of Schleiermacher, London (Hodder & Stoughton), 1890.